W9-CFZ-714

PRACTICAL WISDOM FROM THE BIBLE IN CONTEMPORARY LANGUAGE

Eugene H. Peterson

The Message is a contemporary rendering of the Bible from the original languages, crafted to present its tone, rhythm, events, and ideas in everyday language.

NAVPRESS

BRINGING TRUTH TO LIFE

P.O. Box 35001, Colorado Springs, Colorado 80935

Turn to page 17 for answers to frequently asked
questions about *The Message*.

New Testament Exegetical Consultants:
  Dr. William W. Klein (Chairman)
  Denver Seminary
Dr. Darrell L. Bock
  Dallas Theological Seminary
Dr. Donald A. Hagner
  Fuller Theological Seminary

Dr. Moisés Silva
  Gordon-Conwell Theological Seminary
The Rev. Dr. Rodney A. Whitacre
Trinity Episcopal School for Ministry

Published in association with the literary agency of Alive Communications, 1465
Kelly Johnson Blvd., Suite 320, Colorado Springs, CO 80920.

ISBN 1-57683-210-4

Printed in the United States of America

1 2 3 4 5 6 7 8 9 10 11 12 13 14 15/05 04 03 02 01 00 99

JAMES

W hen Christian believers gather in churches, everything that can go wrong sooner or later does. Outsiders, on observing this, conclude that there is nothing to the religion business except, perhaps, business—and dishonest business at that. Insiders see it differently. Just as a hospital collects the sick under one roof and labels them as such, the church collects sinners. Many of the people outside the hospital are every bit as sick as the ones inside, but their illnesses are either undiagnosed or disguised. It's similar with sinners outside the church.

So Christian churches are not, as a rule, model communities of good behavior. They are, rather, places where human misbehavior is brought out in the open, faced, and dealt with.

The letter of James shows one of the church's early pastors skillfully going about his work of confronting, diagnosing, and dealing with areas of misbelief and misbehavior that had turned up in congregations committed to his care. Deep and living wisdom is on display here, wisdom both rare and essential. Wisdom is not primarily knowing the truth, although it certainly includes that; it is skill in living. For, what good is a truth if we don't know how to live it? What good is an intention if we can't sustain it?

According to church traditions, James carried the nickname "Old Camel Knees" because of thick calluses built up on his knees from many years of determined prayer. The prayer is foundational to the wisdom. Prayer is always foundational to wisdom.

JAMES

1 I, James, am a slave of God and the Master Jesus, writing to the twelve tribes scattered to Kingdom Come: Hello!

FAITH UNDER PRESSURE

Consider it a sheer gift, friends, when tests and challenges come at you from all sides. You know that under pressure, your faith-life is forced into the open and shows its true colors. So don't try to get out of anything prematurely. Let it do its work so you become mature and well-developed, not deficient in any way.

If you don't know what you're doing, pray to the Father. He loves to help. You'll get his help, and won't be condescended to when you ask for it. Ask boldly, believingly, without a second thought. People who "worry their prayers" are like wind-whipped waves. Don't think you're going to get anything from the Master that way, adrift at sea, keeping all your options open.

When down-and-outers get a break, cheer! And when the arrogant rich are brought down to size, cheer! Prosperity is as short-lived as a wildflower, so don't ever count on it. You know that as soon as the sun rises, pouring down its scorching heat, the flower withers. Its petals wilt and, before you know it, that beautiful face is a barren stem. Well, that's a picture of the "prosperous life." At the very moment everyone is looking on in admiration, it fades away to nothing.

Anyone who meets a testing challenge head-on and manages to stick it out is mighty fortunate. For such persons loyally in love with God, the reward is life and more life.

Don't let anyone under pressure to give in to evil say, "God is trying to trip me up." God is impervious to evil, and puts evil in no one's way. The temptation to give in to evil comes from us and only us. We have no one to blame but the leering, seducing flare-up of our own lust. Lust gets pregnant, and has a baby: sin! Sin grows up to adulthood, and becomes a real killer.

So, my very dear friends, don't get thrown off course. Every desirable and beneficial gift comes out of heaven. The gifts are rivers of light cascading down from the Father of Light. There is nothing deceitful in God, nothing two-faced, nothing fickle. He brought us to life using the true Word, showing us off as the crown of all his creatures.

ACT ON WHAT YOU HEAR

Post this at all the intersections, dear friends: Lead with your ears, follow up with your tongue, and let anger straggle along in the rear. God's righteousness doesn't grow from human anger. So throw all spoiled virtue and cancerous evil in the garbage. In simple humility, let our gardener, God, landscape you with the Word, making a salvation-garden of your life.

Don't fool yourself into thinking that you are a listener when you are anything but, letting the Word go in one ear and out the other. *Act* on what you hear! Those who hear and don't act are like

7

those who glance in the mirror, walk away, and two minutes later have no idea who they are, what they look like.

But whoever catches a glimpse of the revealed counsel of God—the free life!—even out of the corner of his eye, and sticks with it, is no distracted scatterbrain but a man or woman of action. That person will find delight and affirmation in the action.

Anyone who sets himself up as "religious" by talking a good game is self-deceived. This kind of religion is hot air and only hot air. Real religion, the kind that passes muster before God the Father, is this: Reach out to the homeless and loveless in their plight, and guard against corruption from the godless world.

THE ROYAL RULE OF LOVE

2 My dear friends, don't let public opinion influence how you live out our glorious, Christ-originated faith. If a man enters your church wearing an expensive suit, and a street person wearing rags comes in right after him, and you say to the man in the suit, "Sit here, sir; this is the best seat in the house!" and either ignore the street person or say, "Better sit here in the back row," haven't you segregated God's children and proved that you are judges who can't be trusted?

Listen, dear friends. Isn't it clear by now that God operates quite differently? He chose the world's down-and-out as the kingdom's first citizens, with full rights and privileges. This kingdom is promised to anyone who loves God. And here you are abusing these same citizens! Isn't it the high and mighty who exploit you, who use the courts to rob you blind? Aren't they the ones who scorn the new name—"Christian"—used in your baptisms?

You do well when you complete the Royal Rule of the Scriptures: "Love others as you love yourself." But if you play up to these so-called important people, you go against the Rule and stand convicted by it. You can't pick and choose in these things, specializing in keeping one or two things in God's law and ignoring others. The same God who said, "Don't commit adultery," also said, "Don't murder." If you don't commit adultery but go ahead and murder, do you think your non-adultery will cancel out your murder? No, you're a murderer, period.

Talk and act like a person expecting to be judged by the Rule that sets us free. For if you refuse to act kindly, you can hardly expect to be treated kindly. Kind mercy wins over harsh judgment every time.

FAITH IN ACTION

Dear friends, do you think you'll get anywhere in this if you learn all the right words but never do anything? Does merely talking about faith indicate that a person really has it? For instance, you come upon an old friend dressed in rags and half-starved and say, "Good morning, friend! Be clothed in Christ! Be filled with the Holy Spirit!" and walk off without providing so much as a coat or a cup of soup—where does that get you? Isn't it obvious that God-talk without God-acts is outrageous nonsense?

I can already hear one of you agreeing by saying, "Sounds good. You take care of the faith department, I'll handle the works department."

Not so fast. You can no more show me your works apart from your faith than I can show you my faith apart from my works. Faith and works, works and faith, fit together hand in glove.

Do I hear you professing to believe in the one and only God, but then observe you complacently sitting back as if you had done something wonderful? That's just great. Demons do that, but what good does it do them? Use your heads! Do you suppose for a minute that you can cut faith and works in two and not end up with a corpse on your hands?

Wasn't our ancestor Abraham "made right with God by works" when he placed his son Isaac on the sacrificial altar? Isn't it obvious that faith and works are yoked partners, that faith expresses itself in works? That the works are "works of faith"? The full meaning of "believe" in the Scripture sentence, "Abraham believed God and was set right with God," includes his action. It's that mesh of believing and acting that got Abraham named "God's friend." Is it not evident that a person is made right with God not by a barren faith but by faith fruitful in works?

The same with Rahab, the Jericho harlot. Wasn't her action in hiding God's spies and helping them escape—that seamless unity of *believing* and *doing*—what counted with God? The very moment you separate body and spirit, you end up with a corpse. Separate faith and works and you get the same thing: a corpse.

WHEN YOU OPEN YOUR MOUTH

3 Don't be in any rush to become a teacher, my friends. Teaching is highly responsible work. Teachers are held to the strictest standards. And none of us are perfectly qualified. We get it wrong nearly every time we open our mouths. If you could find someone whose speech was perfectly true, you'd have a perfect person, in perfect control of life.

A bit in the mouth of a horse controls the whole horse. A small rudder on a huge ship in the hands of a skilled captain sets a course in the face of the strongest winds. A word out of your mouth may seem of no account, but it can accomplish nearly anything—or destroy it!

It only takes a spark, remember, to set off a forest fire. A careless or wrongly placed word out of your mouth can do that. By our speech we can ruin the world, turn harmony to chaos, throw mud on a reputation, send the whole world up in smoke and go up in smoke with it, smoke right from the pit of hell.

This is scary: You can tame a tiger, but you can't tame a tongue—it's never been done. The tongue runs wild, a wanton killer. With our tongues we bless God our Father; with the same tongues we curse the very men and women he made in his image. Curses and blessings out of the same mouth!

My friends, this can't go on. A spring doesn't gush fresh water one day and brackish the next, does it? Apple trees don't bear strawberries, do they? Raspberry bushes don't bear apples, do they? You're not going to dip into a polluted mud hole and get a cup of clear, cool water, are you?

Live Well, Live Wisely

Do you want to be counted wise, to build a reputation for wisdom? Here's what you do: Live well, live wisely, live humbly. It's the way you live, not the way you talk, that counts. Mean-spirited ambition isn't wisdom. Boasting that you are wise isn't wisdom. Twisting the truth to make yourselves sound wise isn't wisdom. It's the furthest thing from wisdom—it's animal cunning, devilish conniving. Whenever you're trying to look better than others or get the better of others, things fall apart and everyone ends up at the others' throats.

Real wisdom, God's wisdom, begins with a holy life and is characterized by getting along with others. It is gentle and reasonable, overflowing with mercy and blessings, not hot one day and cold the next, not two-faced. You can develop a healthy, robust community that lives right with God and enjoy its results *only* if you do the hard work of getting along with each other, treating each other with dignity and honor.

Get Serious

4 Where do you think all these appalling wars and quarrels come from? Do you think they just happen? Think again. They come about because you want your own way, and fight for it deep inside yourselves. You lust for what you don't have and are willing to kill to get it. You want what isn't yours and will risk violence to get your hands on it.

You wouldn't think of just asking God for it,

would you? And why not? Because you know you'd be asking for what you have no right to. You're spoiled children, each wanting your own way.

You're cheating on God. If all you want is your own way, flirting with the world every chance you get, you end up enemies of God and his way. And do you suppose God doesn't care? The proverb has it that "he's a fiercely jealous lover." And what he gives in love is far better than anything else you'll find. It's common knowledge that "God goes against the willful proud; God gives grace to the willing humble."

So let God work his will in you. Yell a loud *no* to the Devil and watch him scamper. Say a quiet *yes* to God and he'll be there in no time. Quit dabbling in sin. Purify your inner life. Quit playing the field. Hit bottom, and cry your eyes out. The fun and games are over. Get serious, really serious. Get down on your knees before the Master; it's the only way you'll get on your feet.

Don't bad-mouth each other, friends. It's God's Word, his Message, his Royal Rule, that takes a beating in that kind of talk. You're supposed to be honoring the Message, not writing graffiti all over it. God is in charge of deciding human destiny. Who do you think you are to meddle in the destiny of others?

Nothing But a Wisp of Fog

And now I have a word for you who brashly announce, "Today—at the latest, tomorrow—we're off to such and such a city for the year. We're going to start a business and make a lot of money." You don't know the first thing about tomorrow. You're nothing but a wisp of fog, catching a brief bit of sun before disappearing. Instead, make it a habit to say, "If the Master wills it and we're still alive, we'll do this or that."

As it is, you are full of your grandiose selves. All such vaunting self-importance is evil. In fact, if you know the right thing to do and don't do it, that, for you, *is* evil.

DESTROYING YOUR LIFE FROM WITHIN

5 And a final word to you arrogant rich: Take some lessons in lament. You'll need buckets for the tears when the crash comes upon you. Your money is corrupt and your fine clothes stink. Your greedy luxuries are a cancer in your gut, destroying your life from within. You thought you were piling up wealth. What you've piled up is judgment.

All the workers you've exploited and cheated cry out for judgment. The groans of the workers you used and abused are a roar in the ears of the Master Avenger. You've looted the earth and lived it up. But all you'll have to show for it is a fatter than usual corpse. In fact, what you've done is condemn and murder perfectly good persons, who stand there and take it.

✟

Meanwhile, friends, wait patiently for the Master's Arrival. You see farmers do this all the time, waiting for their valuable crops to mature, patiently letting the rain do its slow but sure work. Be patient like that. Stay steady and strong. The Master could arrive at any time.

Friends, don't complain about each other. A far greater complaint could be lodged against you, you know. The Judge is standing just around the corner.

Take the old prophets as your mentors. They put up with anything, went through everything, and never once quit, all the time honoring God. What a gift life is to those who stay the course! You've heard, of course, of Job's staying power, and you know how God brought it all together for him at the end. That's because God cares, cares right down to the last detail.

And since you know that he cares, let your language show it. Don't add words like "I swear to God" to your own words. Don't show your impatience by concocting oaths to hurry up God. Just say yes or no. Just say what is true. That way, your language can't be used against you.

PRAYER TO BE RECKONED WITH

Are you hurting? Pray. Do you feel great? Sing. Are you sick? Call the church leaders together to pray and anoint you with oil in the name of the Master. Believing-prayer will heal you, and Jesus will put you on your feet. And if you've sinned, you'll be forgiven—healed inside and out.

Make this your common practice: Confess your sins to each other and pray for each other so that you can live together whole and healed. The prayer of a person living right with God is something powerful to be reckoned with. Elijah, for instance, human just like us, prayed hard that it wouldn't rain, and it didn't—not a drop for three and a half years. Then he prayed that it would rain, and it did. The showers came and everything started growing again.

My dear friends, if you know people who have wandered off from God's truth, don't write them off. Go after them. Get them back and you will have rescued precious lives from destruction and prevented an epidemic of wandering away from God.

Here are some frequently asked questions about *The Message*.

⁓⦚⁓

What will I get from this Bible that I don't get from others?

- It will give you a fresh perspective on the Bible.
- You'll begin to see passages and books as whole units of thought.
- You'll experience the excitement and feeling of the Bible as it sounded to its first readers.
- You'll be able to follow the train of thought much more easily.
- The Bible will seem more alive and understandable.
- You'll encounter many passages you've read hundreds of times before, yet suddenly it will be like reading it for the first time.

What's so different about The Message?

- It's not meant to replace your current version of choice.
- It is designed as a reading Bible.
- It's written in a language that you would use to write a letter to a friend.
- There is no formal language or distracting verse numbers.
- It reads like one of your favorite novels, yet Eugene Peterson works exclusively from the original languages.

How did The Message *begin? And why?*

"While I was teaching a class on Galatians, I began to realize that the adults in my class weren't feeling the vitality and directness that I sensed as I read and studied the New Testament in its original Greek. Writing straight from the original text, I began to attempt to bring into English the rhythms and idioms of the original language. I knew that the early readers of the New Testament were captured and engaged by these writings, and wanted my congregation to be impacted in the same way. I hoped to bring the New Testament to life for two different types of people: those who hadn't read the Bible because it seemed too distant and irrelevant, and those who had read the Bible so much that it had become 'old hat.'"

—*Eugene H. Peterson*

Desiring to communicate the cutting-edge vitality of the Bible to his congregation, Dr. Peterson began to put the Greek text of Galatians into contemporary language. From this seed, *The Message* grew. Working closely with a NavPress senior editor, he spent over two years continuing his creative translation of the New Testament. He then began work on the Psalms and Wisdom books. His work continues today as he is diligently working toward the completion of the entire Bible.

EUGENE PETERSON is a writer and poet. He has authored more than twenty books and is a contributing editor to Leadership Journal.

He is Professor Emeritus of Spiritual Theology at Regent College in Vancouver, British Columbia. Eugene also founded Christ Our King Presbyterian Church in Bel Air, Maryland, where he ministered for twenty-nine years.

How do you make sure **The Message** *is accurately translated?*

A team of exegetical consultants—distinguished professors from various seminaries and colleges—review the text to ensure that it accurately communicates the original Hebrew and Greek.

New Testament Consultants

WILLIAM W. KLEIN—Denver Seminary: CHAIRMAN
DARRELL L. BOCK—Dallas Theological Seminary
DONALD A. HAGNER—Fuller Theological Seminary
MOISÉS SILVA—Gordon-Conwell Theological Seminary
RODNEY A. WHITACRE—Trinity Episcopal School for Ministry

Old Testament Consultants

ROBERT L. HUBBARD—North Park Theological Seminary: CHAIRMAN
ROBERT L. ALDEN—Denver Seminary
RICHARD E. AVERBECK—Trinity Evangelical Divinity School
BRYAN E. BEYER—Columbia Bible College
LAMAR E. COOPER, SR.—Criswell College
PETER E. ENNS—Westminster Theological Seminary
DUANE A. GARRETT—Bethel Seminary
DONALD R. GLENN—Dallas Theological Seminary
PAUL R. HOUSE—Southern Baptist Theological Seminary
V. PHILIPS LONG—Covenant Theological Seminary
TREMPER LONGMAN III—Westmont College
JOHN N. OSWALT—Wesley Biblical Seminary
RICHARD L. PRATT, JR.—Reformed Theological Seminary
JOHN H. WALTON—Moody Bible Institute
PRESCOTT H. WILLIAMS, JR.—Austin Presbyterian Theological Seminary
MARVIN R. WILSON—Gordon College

When will the whole Bible be complete?

- **Prophets—Release October 2000**
  Isaiah, Jeremiah, Lamentations, Ezekiel, Daniel,
  Hosea, Joel, Amos, Obadiah, Jonah, Micah,
  Nahum, Habakkuk, Zephaniah, Haggai,
  Zechariah, Malachi.

- **Pentateuch—Release October 2001**
  Genesis, Exodus, Leviticus, Numbers,
  Deuteronomy.

- **History—Release July 2002**
  Joshua, Judges, Ruth, 1 Samuel, 2 Samuel,
  1 Kings, 2 Kings, 1 Chronicles, 2 Chronicles,
  Ezra, Nehemiah, Esther.

- ***The Message* Bible—Release July 2002**
  The complete Old and New Testament combined
  into one volume.

What are readers of The Message saying about it?

"What a breath of fresh air." SMITHVILLE, TN

"It's tremendous, refreshing, stirring—and a splendid gift." "A cool way to tell God's truth in today's language." LYNCHBURG, VA

"After 30 years of study I finally get it. *The Message* is so easy to read. Chapter after chapter the language relates to where I am in today's world." ERIE, PA

"*The Message* is great for those who have never heard the Bible, as well as for those who have heard it so many times that they cannot hear the meaning anymore." LAFAYETTE, CA

"I honestly couldn't put it down! It is amazingly readable and formatted without verse numbers. You just open it up and read! Wow! It really jumps out at you. I love this version. It isn't my only Bible, but it's the one that gets read the most." PHOENIX, AZ

"I was skeptical when I was given a copy of *The Message*. I thought I would be terribly disappointed! The Opposite has been true. I have not been able to put this book down!" LUBBOCK, TX

What editions are currently available?

 **The New Testament, Psalms & Proverbs**
$22.99 Hardback 1-57683-119-1
$16.99 Paperback 1-57683-120-5
$42 Leather 0-89109-918-2
$22 Pocket Leather 1-57683-022-5

 The Wisdom Books
(Job, Psalms, Proverbs, Ecclesiastes, and Song of Songs)
$14.99 Paperback
1-57683-126-4

 Job
$12 Hardback
0-89109-927-1

 Psalms
$10 Paperback
0-89109-788-0

 Proverbs
$10 Hardback
0-89109-917-4

$5 Pocket Paperback
0-89109-916-6

Stories of Jesus
$12 Hardback
1-57683-183-3

Sayings of Jesus
$12 Hardback
1-57683-104-3

His Unfolding Grace
$12 Hardback
1-57683-107-8

The Message Promise Book
$5 Paperback
1-57683-015-2

Messages for the Heart
$12 Audio
1-57683-038-1

Where can I buy a copy of The Message?

- Call NavPress at 1-800-366-7788
- Visit our website at www.navpress.com
- Bookstores everywhere
- Internet booksellers